T0168464

POEMA

Camino del Sol

A Latina and Latino Literary Series

POEMA

Poems by Maurice Kilwein Guevara

The University of Arizona Press   Tucson

The University of Arizona Press
© 2009 Maurice Kilwein Guevara
All rights reserved

www.uapress.arizona.edu

Library of Congress Cataloging-in-Publication Data
Kilwein Guevara, Maurice.
  Poema : poems / by Maurice Kilwein Guevara.
    p. cm. — (Camino del sol)
  ISBN 978-0-8165-2725-0 (pbk. : acid-free paper)
  I. Title.
PS3561.I4135P63   2009
811'.54—dc22   2008033645

Publication of this book is made possible in part by the proceeds of a
permanent endowment created with the assistance of a Challenge Grant
from the National Endowment for the Humanities, a federal agency.

Manufactured in the United States of America on acid-free, archival-
quality paper containing a minimum of 30% post-consumer waste and
processed chlorine free.

14   13   12   11   10   09   6   5   4   3   2   1

Soy tan pobre ¿qué otra cosa puedo dar?

—Álvaro Carrillo

Contents

I

II

III

IV

I

A man believes he has photographed the hair of the woman he loves, mingled with bits of straw, as she sleeps in a field. But in the developed snapshot there appear a thousand divergent arms, shining fists, weapons; we see that it's the photo of a riot.

—Claude Cahun

Lyric

I snore.

Greedy for the horizon and its multiplication in rain,
I'm digging up the brow of the rust-veined stone,
Howlers in the high trees telling us to move on.
The shadows

Divide your face. Your small hands are wavy in the creek.
I want to paint your fingernails Costa Rican green.
One by one, I want to blow on them.

The white breath of a jet opens the sky.
I want you to open me, Eunice Odio.
I snore.
As I turn on my left shoulder, my bottom leg kicks the cotton sheet.
I want to eat moras out of your palm
And trace the frond shadows focusing
Over the small of your back.

Green line of leaf-cutter ants,
Thread of time-scented molecules,
Poetry is spit and fungus growing underground.

Wake me up, Eunice.

Your lips tumble like the night-red of Arenal.

Your dress on the floor feels aqua-lemon,

The cool skin of orchids.

My mouth is open.

I admit it:

I'm greedy for the entire Pacific Ocean and whales.

I cross the border for roasted iguana and onion.

Tremors at Momotombo. Where are you?

You started, "A woman who was suddenly lost

Because the air wanted her . . ."

What does that mean, Eunice?

I'm snoring,

Little choking sounds.

Please, don't let me sleep past the June hour.

Against Metaphor

for Santiago Calatrava

Chair is not Mine Sweeper

Chives not Tympani

Sweet Potato not Chimes

Tortoise-shell in Heat not the Port of Milwaukee at Quitting Time

I not the Grandson of Carlos Guevara Moreno

Frame not Bolivia with Lavender Mountains

Barrel Hoop not the Acrobatic Girl with Pinned Braids

Dark Moth on the Kitchen Windowsill not Syllable of Julia de Burgos

Walt Whitman not Esprit d'Escalier

Ruana not Memory of Birth not Turning Torso

Clarinet with Reed not Dolphin in Underwater Cavern

Poems not Iron Lung not Kidney Transplantation not Faith Healing

Truth not Unpainted Back Door Half-Open near Cooper's Rock, West Virginia

Ground Squirrel not Swallow not Dry Axle

6 and 496 not Perfect Pitch

Beads of Rainwater Rolling down Pale Leaves of Broccoli not Ellipsis

How then should I explain to you the Undetonated Woman at once on the
banks of Lake Michigan and Texcoco who is my Sailing Ship and White Bird
and Kiss and Blowing Huipil Embroidered with Orange and Lime Threads?

The other word for thesaurus

Is treasure. Or tesoro. For tesoro I mean the toddler who is in a body cast because otherwise his spine may become permanently deformed. I don't believe in God. Look at the bones of his shoulders. He is opening presents on his third birthday and says thank you but wishes the little book were a train named Thomas. For Thomas is another way to say César Vallejo. I'll talk now only if I can turn away. Say this in Quechua or Arabic. There is a dead man or teenaged girl in the mountains witnessed by roads. There is infinity in the skull small enough for beaks to enter. In the reflected stars we each touch the letters hidden there.

Click

Close the wooden door until it clicks,
exile sleeping children and downstairs
coughing of congestive heart failure.
In the bed a sheen of mint
balm on her lips. If you lift her hair,
at the nape, if you lift here,
it's shaded air under a coffee tree,
rolling darkness of the central valley.
Turn her hip. Reverse the sail
of a skiff whose glass hull is a human face
staring down at a school of electric
fish. Teeth click. Kiss the skin
of her clavicle, little key turning
from sternum to scapula. See the wings
of the stingrays as shadows. Shadows
of thighs and arms on the fraying counterpane. Low jet's
buzzing the windows in their wooden frames.
Touch her where her arm bends, pocket
of heated molecules. Ravel. Come
before the mew beneath you rattles open.

Someone Complaining Around Here

Someone's changed the pillowcases and feathers,
removed the roof of our house because I guess
I complained
under my breath
one dusk four years ago:
daylight's
getting darker, diabetic, congestive,
more particulates, more water molecules
congregating in the bruised sky, rust
streaks above the factories and mangled freeways.
Without telling me someone simply removed
Thursdays and shortened November by two
vertebrae, then added twenty-one-and-a-third miles
between any two points. AAA's stopped road service
at night in the state of Indiana: it's too tenebrous.
The wintering birds, once stoic with ragweed seeds,
are all in law school now. Except my love, who's Cree.
I don't fault her.
Nevertheless, I worry my shouting love and I
have grown to sleep through even the late summer storms
with lightning,
the whispering of electric torture,
the shearing wind,
the endless whining motors of our epoch, the bat chirps.

One Star

Wind-barbed night over your shoulder in a field up north—
no moon or streetlights, no gunshots or blinking jets—
you begin to run, to sprint beyond the ruined farmhouse,
to pull the line as far as it will go, and finally to feel the snap
of the dark-blue invisible kite, one star, fishhook of light.

Joan Brossa as the Emerald Moth Discharging Energy

Spinnerets of fiber optics, release:
you're always at the end of your line
or begin to descend
from the upper
left-hand corner of the window.
Look at the tomato plants on the other side of the glass,
the little yellow flowers,
the diamond leaves of the nightshade,
pendulous red and copper fruit,
the sunlit green stems with pale micro-bristles, cilia.
Jailer in chiaroscuro,
prisoner of the cellar,
student of the light switch,
stargazer through a cataract of dusty glass,
drowsy lepidopterist.

This is the strophe starring Joan Brossa
as the panicked emerald moth,
Joan Brossa en España, ensnared,
Joan Brossa being eaten by a wet strawberry,
Joan Brossa writing POEMA on a clear lightbulb,
Joan Brossa swimming the butterfly,

Joan Brossa a shape of color balancing
on a blush orchid in tierra caliente,
Joan Brossa at twilight staring up at Gederme,
Joan Brossa's statue with mountainous feet and legs,
genitalia and twisting torso transparent liquid glass
with buzzing filament.

What wakes you
just as you begin to dream of Heidegger
in a clouded field of summer chives?

Two Poets This Morning and Me in My Red Boxer Shorts

The gray-brown hare I carried horizontally at the end of the spade
was headless,
the dark,
jewel-red opening
of the chest
summery with larvae.
The night before my wife smelled fish.
A foot fell off
with a bit of fur
softly on the grass.
Elizabeth Bishop was weeding in our garden in a sienna blouse,
scrutinizing an archipelago of tiny, light-green thistles.
She was singing um pouco de português
when Bernadette Mayer said *C'mere*
and pointed into the hole.
I was dragging a flat rake across the lawn to push the dirt back.
C'mere, look at that erection.
She meant what was left of the spine,
almost vertical,
a cervical shade of white.
Could it hear the micro-sonic frenzy of diaphanous wings?
Two vertebrae stood exposed
even
after
my first steady pass covered the bulk of the thorax.

Mr. Berryman Has Injured His Foot in Putting Out a Fire

—Samuel Hazo

After her sweating over their federal taxes
& Mr. Berryman

On the wood floor
Yellow jacket of his pulp Blake
Blossoms fire
This beside the ninth very dry
Martini
The undergrad paper
On Angra Mainyu
Nervy tin
Crotch of his tipsy ash

Johnny Smith for whom the funny world
Hung dark
In black-stockinged feet

Stamped his experienced foot
Where Hell
Fired up through a ferret hole in the knotted oak

O how his ginny sock grew bloody
And glass pricked his merry blistered

If Vietnam a pastoral
Sunned by falling napalm
Hazard
Yesterday's three twisting from bed sheets at Gitmo
Were "an act of asymmetrical warfare waged against us"

In the City of Havana, El Porvenir

They say the icy winds actually started two weeks earlier, blowing from the cracked nostrils and bleeding mouth of a roan horse, supine and abandoned on the frozen plains of Kansas, the breath (visible from satellites) tinged a sky-blue and tunneling in horizontal columns as it drilled toward the Caribbean.

But it was Doña Marisol who first saw it, she who likes to keep her lips painted a little orange like a poppy in case who knows she might have an unexpected visitor and it's nice to feel pretty especially if you're seventy-eight next month. Doña Marisol, whose mouth even this late February night is painted bright, she who lives on the top floor of a tenement that was once a handsome edifice, she who is collecting her laundry from the rooftop very late because she had to finish that damn novel to see whether the young thing from the country would be consumed by the flame of that rich so-and-so—the same Doña Marisol cannot believe how cold the air is, how pinned to the clothesline her sheets and homemade dresses and underpants are starched with the thinnest coating of ice, how the cloudy sky is suddenly puffs of light falling on her and melting, how within minutes the roof overlooking the sluggish sea is covered in snow, how the little swirls of blowing white are filling even her clay flowerpots . . .

By the next morning there are more than three feet of snow covering all parts of the city, over Vedado, over la Habana Vieja, over Necrópolis Cristóbal

Colón, over Pogolotti and Belén de Marianao, even over the last house on the street without a name. The barrios are beginning to lose power as it snows into the afternoon. In spite of this, a young man whose skin is the color of fresh coffee continues to play his alto saxophone, the notes muted through the brass bell filling again with snow.

No one knows at what point someone decides to cover in a woolen blanket the statue of José Martí holding that little boy made of metal and pointing.

Bright Pittsburgh Morning

This must happen just after I die: At sunrise
I bend over my grandparents' empty house in Hazelwood
and pull it out of the soft cindered earth by the Mon River.
Copper tubing and electric lines hang down like hairs.
The house is the size of a matchbox. I sprinkle bits
of broken pallets, seeded grass, fingernails, and tamarack
needles in the open door of the porch. I scratch a Blue Tip
and blow vowels of fire through the living room,
the tunneled hallway. Flames run up the wooden stairs.
I put my ear beside the hot kitchen window
to hear the crackling voices of cupboards and walls.
I flip the welder's mask:
Sun off the rectangular glass, a rose glint before the white torch.

I'll never eat another rarebit as long as I live

Where was the small bone under the round mole on my right hand?

When I touched the cranberry bruise, I remembered me at her wake.

Later, as I drove on, the silhouette of her corpse became the

      Appalachians.

Then, weeks later, my left femur was gone.

I checked the pantry, of course.

At the humid patriotic concert, I suddenly noticed deafness in both

      ears.

When the other femur disappeared, even limping was out of the question.

My brother was kind enough to push me with a broom.

He pushed me to the kitchen where I mushed a bit of banana.

He pushed me to the sunny bus stop and dropped some nickels in my palm.

He swept my thin, rubbery legs closer to my chin.

But all that friction eventually caused me terrible rug burns.

I said, *what did you say the guy said?*

Then, before my brother could answer, my ribs were being filched.

By Labor Day, my cervical vertebrae were history.

My head lolled to one side, a spring house flower.

My brother is a kind man but grew tired of pushing me around.

I can't blame him. He said, *Can sciatica give off an electrical smell?*

He began to make excuses: *Sorry, I have to go to so-and-so's viewing.*

I tried to redouble my efforts; unfortunately, it was on the fire

      escape.

I rolled.

I tried to soldier on.

But the house cat began to nip at my cornea.

Broken blood vessels blossomed when I blinked.

I tried to scare the cat away.

But you need ribs to roar and at least one acromioclavicular joint.

And there is little dignity without cheekbones.

Shadowy claw, teeth, backhoe:

Oh yes, then the calvarium came unhinged.

II

History is the learning of spectacular consistency privately and learning it

alone and when more comes they receive.

—Gertrude Stein

At rest

We are not merely more weary because of yesterday, we are other.

—Samuel Beckett

La casa arde,
la abuelita se peina.

Streaks of spinning planetary stones,
the horse's hooves
skating
down the canyon path,
another tourist on her back.

How long will he hold his breath under water for me?

Humpback males
in July
breaching
halfway between
Puerto López
e
Isla de la Plata.

How long will he hold his breath in the water for me?
How long will he not live in the deaf dark wet mother-sack?
How long will he not be born?

Listen to that:
Nails biting into the horse's hooves.

Is this the augury of the equine fetus?

You ask too many questions.
From now on, you may only ask one question a day.

From the fish to the krill.
From krill to the orange clown fish.
Fish to krill.
Krill to school.
Going down to the underwater depth of groundlessness,
will he kill himself for me?

Shale formations in the desert, tall as twin towers,
an almost unseen choza at the bottom of the canyon.
In the open window, the grandmother is combing out her thick, iron hair.
Transistor radio battery on steel wool:
This is not the United States of America or México.
This is not the Hopi Nation.
The gray wood of the hut begins to burn
while the hummingbird beside the sweet water,
speckled jade breast,
seems
almost
still.

History

In the early days of the last century a Jesus Christ lizard ran out of my great-grandmother Policarpa's pink, almost cerise, vagina and across the wide Guayas River. It was never found. This was quite an embarrassment to our family. To her dying day, despite the sailor's Brownie camera photograph, bisabuelita Policarpa denied that such a thing had ever happened.

This past June along the Río Frío in Nicaragua I spotted a reptile egg in the wild. Beside the errant water, I knelt and listened to the arc of the shell. I closed my eyes and saw antique loudspeakers, crackling. The leader had just entered the balcony where a man was singing a bolero.

The presidential candidate of 1956 wore an eggshell-white European suit, Florsheims, a gold Rolex. He was showing the back of his right hand and his white teeth to the enormous crowd that had gathered in the northern suburbs of Guayaquil. The leader released a ruby-colored lizard from his left sleeve, and it zipped down the side of the building. There was a roar of approval. A mosquito was removing blood from my ankle. Still, I couldn't stop listening.

How beautiful it was: the bolero, the guitar, the orchid-pink voice of Julio Jaramillo.

Poema cubano con cara vieja

La red

Pared

Pared

La red

Poema cubano

Con cara café

Face note

Net of creases

Come come

Comes

Comes out

Crops up

A stogie

Sprouts

A brown stump

Faces out

Pores

Cinnamon

Time-net a brown face

Pores

Becomes

De la pared

Un puro

Comes out

A brown face

Crops up

Out of the white

Outcomes

Out of the white plaster

A leathered rolling

Cheekbones slope of forehead

Looks down

And comes a brown face

You

A brown face comes out of the white

You

Out of the wall

Brown pores

A galaxy

Damp old puro

Eyes hooded

Looking down

A brown face comes out of the white plaster, stump of puro in his mouth

Filching Freud

swirling thru the hot humming

opening

Opa Sig-

mund mouth O

burning alive (again)

finger in palate

cancer of the roof

listen buddy, why so quiet?

Grandpa gave me pocket money

for the rocking yellow snowy streetcar

filthy Vienna in 1936 is flooded Pittsburgh

if tambor yoruba

roasted yellow pepper sky

while fires

are burning in the sea

jackdaws drilling the Caspian

oil beads, air a string of pearls

fingering the hole

of cigars

the most savory word in the Empire is ameliorate

or salacious

or fry me, you lug

not Barrett's esophagus

not fungus
not rickety sphincter
nor friable spoor
let's say he kept his rims
of anacoluthon
in medicine-bottle blue
vials (with raised dots)
his cocaine
on the morel-stained mantle in the crater where he dreamed
him sucking
and a little choking
opened Pandora's box
at 2:34 on the ceiling
wet down, my

waylaying
my pinkest hatch
did you hear the papered windows?

the casket store went under

What Baby Gertrude Heard

I only saw it from the air so what can I say except that I was born in Alleghany.
—G.S., 1935

a

Almost daylight crib light barred owl declaiming, "The morning glories are
ravenous. The ravens are mourning. The glories are blaring their trumpets
insidious etcetera soot." I will Pittsburgh my infancy. I will Allegheny all
losses and windy cabbage leaves beyond the trellised window where aftershave
walks away as black hair after he dangles shoelaces from polished black
shoes over me. Periods as soot falling on a crib sheet. Think it. Remember it.
Pittsburgh it as the iron horses carry you into the mountains.

b

Taste of cherry pulp.
Smear of cherry red,
faced.
Tear of bleary salt.
Waste of stems and inky pits.
She is she who is cold a gold bracelet on my cheek.
Don't you try? Wrong wrong wrong.
How do you spell a pair a pare of glasses a pear of shoes a chair of
legs made of cherry wood. You don't even get the same misspelling right.
Smelling is thinking.

Don't cry, remember, let the nap go away, fill your nappy with Carnegie if you musk.

I will Pittsburgh my infancy.

A bird with mint feathers is lyrical and, therefore, is said entirely to Allegheny.

I will Allegheny all losses down the river in a paper boat made of history.

c

All rivers lead to the Ohio. A book is door to a forest.

One bituminous crow caw-cawed all through filthy mines and mills: 1874 is six moths of history because it wears polished shoes or muddy boots not to mention horseshoes which aftershave tinkles with after work. Because it changes baby Gertrude who is changed by glamour it grammars history.

d

I will Pittsburgh my infancy.

I'll Allegheny all losses away.

Night syntax of fireflies lighting the cherry-bruised window.

Temporal and verb confusion, morning glories closing lavender cigars.

Frick it. If I'm wrong, then I'll just have to make it up. Steel it.

Soup for an Oligarch

Using a cordless drill, stir the air in a clockwise motion until you hear trains where previously there'd been a swamp with lemon-soft birds and their graceless squawk. Keep stirring until the charcoal clouds over the pot begin to rain. Imagine a future in which you can see the features of your face arranged in the curling bark of towering trees corralling the entrance of the drained plot and park that will bear your name. Cut carrots and chives to the size of fingers. Avoid corn and tomato and plantain; use cilantro only if some shit-smelling so-and-so manages to press the nape of your neck with the cold-flat side of a machete. Otherwise, wear white turtlenecks and raise your daughters to answer either in French or in English. Above all, invest heavily in the miniaturization of pigs. When the gardener isn't looking, swirl your best cream into the pot and sprinkle with capers. Institute a network of radio stations. Play boleros and novelas. Play Chan Chan. Play Rayito de luna. Play Corona de lágrimas. Grind the orange-yellow flowers of a thousand zucchini fields into paste and incorporate slowly. To season with bromide, scratch the temples of your scalp. When the sows are small as beetles, toss a handful into the pot. They'll swim counterclockwise for centuries in spite of the titanium ladle and the lightning and the waterspouts. Serve in bowls of polished bone in the many-mirrored dining room where even alone you are a multitude.

At the Podium

While uniformed corpses fly home from the desert
latest of windy May
the moment of the President's great thrumming
coincides with the Japanese beetle
crawling so far into his tunneled ear
that even a flashlight or match couldn't sun the dark-
orange and speckled wings
lifting the medieval cape
in warning
In that twisting shell
in his inner ear echoes
of alcazars and shipwrecks
still burning under columns of water
of hooves and exploding sand
of propeller engines earthbound
voices beginning to turn
and descend

Below

I wish I could tell you how it is
under the copper skin of the lake hidden by pines:
living with war on clear days,
curves of reptile eggs
emerge from the silt bed and glow
like tiny fox skulls. Swallows dip
and hummingbirds feed
at your open mouth. Apple yellow or cream city,
more names are blowing from the trees.

The Exegesis

Plan Colombia funds the aerial spraying of coca and opium fields with Roundup,
the broad-spectrum herbicide patented by Monsanto. . . . (Agent Orange,
interestingly, was also a Monsanto product.)
—George Monbiot

Washing clothes by the river, Luzmilda's eyes burn. Water. Washing.
She beats the white blouse that balloons over the wide, flat stone. GPS
triangulates—electron data stream to the squadron of shining nozzles on
each wing. They, like men, release. Ton by ton and time again, the buzzing
blue sky atomizes. I think of ice crystals shimmering in the air over the Mon
or Hue or Potomac, a million knives rotating through space. Eyes contract.
The child, waiting in the globe of water buried in Luzmilda, turns. Choking,
she wrings the river water from the bloated cloth. And faraway the television
warns us to beware of unmoored Saracens in crop dusters.

Ésta es una crónica de indias.

This plan fulfills the bestiary of olden times.

Witness the thick thighs of the prostrate Yolanda, sun bleeding from her to
the Magdalena.

Sudden blisters and rashes on the backs and the arms of the twins, Nora and
Vero.

Witness Rodolfo born with no mouth.

And this one is called María Teresa. Use that stethoscope to listen to the damaged iambs inside her chest.

The whine of the plane recedes beyond the scar of electric lines.

Luzmilda pins the sleeveless blouse that wants to fly.

In the tarpaper coop a cock with two beaks is pecking his way out of the dark shell.

Blue Dress of Chiquinquirá

The women took turns scrubbing her only dress in a metal basin,
the room lit by forearms and fists
pressing into the ribs of the washboard.
Whiff of vinegar. The hem
finally stopped leaking its blood shadows.
Her hair rinsed with water from a white enamel pitcher.
Can't say where they took the infant body on the spade,
the purpled head and torso sweated to the dish towel.
Outside the day was bright and with wind.
The cordillera in the distance pine-dark,
charcoal above the dress
wanting to fly backwards from the clothesline.

A found poem with translations

(Oaxaca, 2004)

Graffiti en un muro blanco
con pintura negra de aerosol:

Advertencia en un autobús
con negrita:

Hoy estoy orgulloso
de tener el color de la
tierra, de mi cultura
y de vivir en este
bello planeta . . .

AL **INDI**vidu**O** QUE SEA SORPRENDIDO
POR NUESTROS VIGILANTES RAYANDO,
PINTANDO O MALTRATANDO ESTA
UNIDAD SERÁ CONSIGNADO ANTE LAS
AUTORIDADES COMPETENTES APARTE DE
PAGAR LOS DAÑOS OCASIONADOS.

ATENTAMENTE, LA DIRECTIVA

Graffiti on a white wall
with black spray paint:

Warning on a bus
with boldface:

Today I am proud
to have the color of the
earth, of my culture
and to live on this
exquisite planet . . .

THE **INDI**VIDUAL THAT IS SURPRISED
BY OUR GUARDS DRAWING ON,
PAINTING, OR VANDALIZING THIS
BUS WILL BE TURNED OVER TO THE
APPROPRIATE AUTHORITIES IN ADDITION
TO BEING FORCED TO PAY FOR **AN**Y
DAMAGES.

SINCERELY, THE MANAGEMENT

New Year's Day, 2006

The desert is burning.

On television they show the lizards on fire pedaling out of view. At eye-level the smoke takes the liquid shape of a bird photographed. The rusty steers are panicked, rioting past the hedges orange with wind. O, Texas and Oklahoma, the prophets have not abandoned you. Out of bone and pine, we will build an ark to dray your dead. Whatever was written on flash paper is now a white spot too bright to be filmed.

5:25 a.m. on August 7, 1957
Nevada Test Site, 19 Kilotons

Who is he, second over from the lower
right corner, hunched in fatigues like the rest?
Despite shielding shut eyes in the crook of his sleeve,

he sees the glowing ulna and radius of his left arm
crossed by the small belled bones of his pitching hand.

Red Brow of Moon

for Arn Chorn-Pond

I play clearest flute in the camps
of the Khmer Rouge
to cover the courtyard
of sudden screams
This is how I survive

When the Vietnamese invade
and the Americans bomb
my stringed kim and flute are lost

Now I bear a rifle as green flames
of malaria rise from me
I am almost always hungry

So many monkeys in the jungle
their eyes everywhere
To kill one openly
would mean my swift death

Only when a baby macaque
solitary and curious
wanders close enough to play

do I grab and pin him beneath me
until all his furred air
is gone

I wait for secret night
then smoke the infant over a pit of leaves and bark
my white teeth finally tearing
the tender striated meat
of the thighs

What high notes
would have breathed
through the hollow of that small white bone?

Gristle of stars and red brow of moon
they who've shown me fruit and streams
what kind of cousin have I become?

Then, poema asks

What was her middle name?
Was it Yolanda?
Was it airy like Josefina?
From which side of media res did she fall?
Were those huascas growing at the side of the train station?
By which tree, fig or eucalyptus,
did we bury the assault rifles and grenades?
What did you see?
Was it a red-winged blur?
What is the color when teeth are burned?
Did the corn butterfly seek out the invisible trail of grenadine?
Where did her earring go?
Did it fall into the green carpet?
What's that a shadow of,
flying over the baked trucha and twisted lemon in the patio?
Did you ask?
Why does their money always smell of jet fuel?
Whose black shoe was abandoned in haste outside her window?
What was her first name?
Where did she first kiss you?
Now can you smell the almojábanas from the mountain?
Why would anyone build such a thing?
At what altitude does blue-silver turn into emerald?
Everyone is laughing after the phlebotomist's funeral.
Everyone.
Who broke the glass, the chicha on the white stone?

III

What you are picturing, if I can see into your mind a little bit, is at some point where we're standing now there were a bunch of very little people sitting around and cooking a very little elephant.

—Bob Simon, *60 Minutes*

Little people sitting around roasting little elephants

hunting again another rat bite ah not another rat bite yep another rat bite eat some trunk some good stringy trunk I love it when it's crunchy did you kill it hey sit away from the wind move over there more tree what more tree huh throw on more tree okay oh that weed smells real good throw on that weed yep right on those fat bubbles so I took it up by the tail and whacked its head on a stone and said ha-ha Great Grandmother you can't fool me you miserable three-eyed rat move over there by the stump in the purple shade then little drops of blood came out of her eyes and I said quit your crying Great Grandmother my grandfather was a weta giant weta devil of the night we used to say I guess you have to move across the creek then you do stink hear that hear what listen what the steps of the oafs they're walking around I hate oafs they steal your weeds they have penises the size of little elephants and they smell like him me too I hate oafs well I had sex once with a long-waisted oaf in the rain and I have to say it was really good look at the fat bubbles on that gut I can see a face can you see a face I see a million stars from the other world no it's a face you're right it's got a pimply forehead the furry oaf I see it too see the pores that open and close see the streaky blue tusks I think it's frowning should I get the digital camera

Pets

pa' Gilberto

It's just me and the ants in my apartment.

I almost never kill them, though I talk to them so much, late at night, about old movies y mi herida isleña, that some have fled to live in the dumpster at the corner pharmacy. Some have left tragic notes or tracks as they trudged through my soft butter on route to the windowsill.

I give the ones who stay and their children names: my sweet Cuqui, Roberto, Doña Pura, Horner, McQueen, Fiona, Juana la Loca, Bucky, Esmeralda, Dorita, Dorita la Segunda, Vlad Tepes, Piel Canela, Sal, Julia, St. John of the Cross . . .

The sugar ants are zealots; the pharaohs a winged frenesí swarming from under the kitchen sink as July sun skins the sidewalk. The carpenter ants cross the branch that touches my bedroom window. I masturbate and smile.

God is Brazilian.

What white chocolate legs and behind have descended the fire escape!

On my cotton sheets, Julia de Burgos and Manuel Puig are scaling the eastern face of the cordillera.

My neighbor's apartment smells like California. It's morning.

Helicopters: the media are landing, antennae going up.

Let's not beatify John Paul II or Mother Teresa or even Margarita Carmen Cansino.

Instead, let it be Cuqui, who is carrying in her mandible the wreckage of Horner's body over the linoleum and doorjamb to the tropics of my yellow bathmat.

Long Time Ago in Chicago John Prine Used to Be My Friend's Mailman

My friend learned one day about a year ago that he had a malignant tumor growing at the back of his left eye, near the optic nerve. A doctor pricked his sclera twice with a long needle, requiring stitches; my friend endured 17 radiation treatments over 17 consecutive weekdays, was the child of holocaust survivors, lost his hair for a while, now has tiny spots in his eyebrow and beard permanently burnt off. For some reason he started wearing a Swatch with a milky cataract lens that makes it impossible to know the time of day. Yesterday he saw a thief run out of a suburban supermarket and down the street with a half gallon of soy milk. Who would steal a half gallon of soy milk? Store workers chased after the man; tackling him, they got all creamy and bloody on the sidewalk.

It makes me want to kiss the thief, Jesus, Joseph, and Mary.

Hector the Colombian Who Butchered the Hair of Juan Ramón

You don't know him? Oh, I figured cause he's Colombian too.
I don't get my hair cut from him no more. Used to.
Used to sit down with him in his shop over on
Lincoln Avenue, and he cut my hair, I guess he cut my hair
like maybe twenty twenty-five times, you know for least ten years,
y fueron cortes de pelo de calidad buena.
See the thing is Hector the Colombian he can bullshit so much
you need waders after a while, him talking about his village in the Andes,
and his mother who wears a crown of thorns cause she's a
super-duper Catholic lady and sees angels in the Tupperware,
and his bother that's a narcoleptic mechanic, and his six sisters in Colombia
who is so beautiful they still ain't married, and he says
that's the difference between Colombia and every other country in the planet
is how beautiful the Colombian women is, etcetera. But the last time I got my
hair cut
by Hector he looked terrible like he ain't slept in a week,
and I can smell the aguardiente through the cheap cologne and gold chains.
Snip snip clip clip he starts up again on how perfect like an emerald
ripped out of the belly of the mountain the Colombian women is clip clip.
Now he starts crying, saying God the Almighty and/or Jesus Christ and even
the Holy Mother is jealous of Colombia because the Colombian women is so
beautiful

like gold shimmering in the sunshine, and God's jealousy is the reason

why Colombia has earthquakes and mudslides and more blood than a butcher

shop

clip clip clip when out of the blue he says *Who am I kidding? She left me*

porque

yo soy un verdadero pendejo and I drink too much and I'm a mess and a bad

person

clip clip, and I start feeling the hot tears falling on my head and neck drip clip,

and I give a quick peek at the mirror and it's a mess. He's fucking up big time,

cutting big ugly bald shapes into my scalp like I got a dog disease,

and it's all uneven clip drip with drops of blood. *The problem, Juan Ramón,*

is I am afraid I am too democratic and love all the women equal,

but for some reason they don't feel the same way about democracy

as I do clip clip. But I say, Hector look man my head's all fucked up, chingado,

you fucked up my head man check it out, and he wipes his eyes, puts the

scissors

and comb down by his side, and I say I ain't paying for that shit.

That's a shit job you done,

and he says in a low, empty voice: *You're right, Juan Ramón.*

You look the way I feel. This one is on me, totalmente gratis.

Las cucarachas pintadas

What requires the greatest precision is the neck loop for the floss leash because above all I want to keep the painted cockroaches breathing for when you take them home after the parades and fireworks: The soldiers in camouflage fatigues, the nun beetle, the two waitresses in hairnets, the surgeon—a spray of blood on his blue gown, the magician with termites up her sleeve, the patriotic welder, the frocked beadle pacing in circles around that little girl's turquoise shoes . . .

The roaches, great actors, are larger than silver dollars. They're surprisingly hard to keep alive. They want to bellow and fall forward on their knees like horses in some cinema cavalry. They want you to remember their branded scars and yellow saddles.

The Sound of Glass is Unmistakable

I'm sitting on a rock in the shade cast by a prickly bush, thinking about the political theory that separated Santander from Bolívar, when I see on the farther ridge a team of horses pulling a long cart that holds a rectangular mirror the size of a movie screen. There's no teamster guiding the yoked horses over the rough and pitched road. It's as if they orient themselves over the landscape by the scent of a shared history. Who feeds them? By what streams do they spend their nights dreaming of a vast confederation of unified states? I wonder as the horses begin trotting more erratically, causing the cinematic glass to jerk.

I see the galleon on which my ancestors escaped from the southern ports of Spain; I see the torsos of Muísca hoeing in a field and slipping off the screen; I see a village of people covered in mud, sliding in the barro, some dancing and bloody and hooded; I see El Tiempo on fire and storefront windows breaking. In all that blurring and shaking, I see a tapestry of red and yellow roses through the milky windows of a greenhouse.

The horses are now in full revolt over the near ridge, at the precipice of the antepasados. The blonde one drags her hind left hoof in the dirt as though she's a cartographer; another begins to gallop; the copper nag high steps it in my direction; while the lead horse, tallest and muscled, chest bright with sweat, leaps into the air with ecstasy.

Sisters, brothers, cousins, uncles, even my mother who normally avoids the atomic sunlight like a movie star, scurry out of a hundred holes to witness the splintered cart and mangled horses, the twin condors circling, the shards of blue sky everywhere.

Pepenador de palabras

Landscape, landfill: from a couple hills away with papers flying and ink-beaked gulls I'm a scavenger rooting about, picker of words, new father trailed by a long cotton sack, Nobody, now a humpback: reader, be careful: intensifiers combust: it's easy to lose your footing: noxious puddles of common nouns red as brake fluid: bottles and fins and the detritus of feathers: iridescent condoms, bloated cardboard: the leg bones of pig and cow I can resell to the soup factory for bullion: bending with her little sleepy weight from dawn until scudding clouds darken the late horizon: dull ache in the back of my thighs turning to numbness as I hunker with tweezers to fill one of four glass vials clipped to my breast pocket: *scry, emunctory, sugared, tic, comma, priapism*: once I dreamed of Remedios Varo in a hammock between trees and a stream: wake up: that slope is where they slide and dump the near-dead fish without permission after closing time: you fall there, you go under for good: the sun at noon chomps at your neck: once I opened a yellow garbage bag stamped with the insignia of the National Library, cut the corded muslin: finger-tagged, it was the desiccated arm of Cervantes clutching a rusted sword: strata and skin: who knew the next day from a fruit crate I'd hear her infant cry: wrap song to my back: bring her home to the sound of boiling water: constant wing-flap of tarpaper: Lucero.

Poema with orange, black-edged wings

Outside a cabin
in Indiana,
Pennsylvania,
I open delicately
the envelope
made of wax paper
and tilt it
toward my pointing finger,
the one I once slipped
into the wound
at the side of his body.

The Monarch's
at first
thin as a slit,
then pulsing south:
verse,
verse,
solar panels open
at the vertex of a tree,
at the tip of a pyramid,
at the torn lip of the aortal mouth
that I, Huitzilopochtli,
have kissed a thousand times.

Let's

They wondered in bed: What if every time we kissed,
someone far away—bending or sleeping—went blind?

This didn't stop them from kissing or biting or seeing on
some afternoons bison or gravestones or teeth in the clouds.

He moved his things into her bleached lighthouse by the lake
some distance away. She asked him never to shave, and his face

became a dark hourglass. With groceries or empty-handed they kissed,
sometimes twice on each step. Helix of steam, she sipped coffee

or nibbled chocolate until the rats, like circus artists without a net,
somehow found their way from the sewerage processing plant

to the telephone wire that entered through their kitchen window.
Some neurologist—with Bell's, I hear—suggested a cell phone,

so he bent his torso through the leaded panes and, in the prism of late
summer light, severed

the line. They never had children; they never had oxen or dogs to
summon home for supper or salt. He grew tall and taller, gaunt,

his lime-white beard long like Whitman's or mine. The woman I love,
sum of my fears, fell deaf one day. Two teens had kissed in Jaipur.

Rata's Preamble

My infancy was pale skin and a series of fairly blind vibrations as I curled
and re-curled for greater warmth into a fist of other half-fingers, sisters and
brothers of the same litter. I have no memory of the rodent sperm from which
I came, the ovum, the embryo, the womb, which even then we called "vientre,"
the contractions (constrictions) squeezing us down the muscled sleeve—¡Ay,
qué vaina!—where my sister Sara said she swore she heard the sea and the
strings of a tiple and the agitated neighing of a seahorse. This is, of course,
before we lived in the apartment; before I learned to shave to make myself
hairless once again; before I went to work at a desk in Bogotá and later in
a ditch in Pittsburgh; before Cementos Boyacá grew to become one of the
largest construction firms in the Americas; before jade; before prescription
lenses; before the stolen jackhammer; before the culture of poisons and
mausoleums; before I knew a thing of Málaga, la Habana, Schopenhauer, or
of Jaipur; before the disappeared.

We were a cache of thirteen baby rats born underground in a field of onions,
near Sogamoso; fourteen, actually, because I chose never to forget our sister
Rosita, who was born with a hole in the left auricle of her heart, which left
a subcutaneous, swirling pink stain on her chest. I heard my mother eat her
almost as soon as she died so there would be more milk. Ours would be a
history of chronic needs.

Native Mussels

Under the Allegheny
kidney failure from mills and farms

the water is cool
and glaucous
and the water column moves

in the Clarion
mine acids and heavy metals

tiny moons of oxygen
rolling to
the river mussels
the pink muckets
the clubshells
the pigtoes

the cool water moves in
    and goes out

food of macroscopic
leaf
and flecks of berry

of milt and drab light

of wood and soft

fish bone

go in

  and out

to pocketbooks

and riffleshells

at French Creek

dark motes of human sewage

by the packed sand

at the bottom of the river

West of Eliza Furnace

This is
a man who scratches a match on the stony floor
with snow falling outside the cathedral windows
and watches the strips of newsprint
turn to moth wings at dawn
swirling inside the woodstove

This is
every jade and black and white or medicine-bottle blue
dot on the wings of a living butterfly
magnified 3x through a glass pitcher of water
on a white table in the sun

This is
my tongue on the evergreen sweat beading over
your nipple your thumbnail sparking the nerve-
web of my sphincter
my preening cardinal we are heat lightning
we're the dream of evaporation

This is the diadem
the bullet made in the hide
of the buck as he fell by railroad ties

now hanging on the starless porch

and twisting

north winds

spiders of snow landing on his brown eyes

Cage

With my jade and pebbled hide, my fleas and magnificent
Talons, why have I long cooped under this iron
Bridge in Kittanning on the Allegheny?

See the green bottle flies over the giant catfish
Rotting on a rock, General Armstrong's hoofed
Men swarming down a hillside with smoke.

Notice how thin my tongue is between my beak,
And pink, the same pink that edges
The ovate clouds just after rush hour.

Look up. In spite of the roar of Exxon trucks,
The whine of motorcycles, the pigeons in the rafters
Line up in syntax with the nesting swallows.

The mother bats ricochet through coordinates
Of mosquitoes, gnats, bluish moths by the bank.
I drag the day's net of mussels and books over the shoals

To my niche under the bridge. I suck in the cool
Slime of the bivalves, I savor the ligaments that tie
Vowels to living bone. I sing for the butchered deities,

For the infants floating in the cattails, I curse
The moon awake with words, hiss away the feral eyes.
I release this flying cage into the darkened world.

IV

The sky is a vast inverted bowl of blue;

about the circling rim the furnaces

are emptying into it like yellow rivers.

—Haniel Long

At Sunrise, Oaxaca

Scat-brown the coyote with teats clamps the rooster's limp
neck and peeks at Ernesto who in a few moments
a half mile down the road is picking berries
that will dye the thread for the tapete's crown,
three spheres of blood over the white chest of feathers.

Teusaquillo, 1989

Eleven bombs had gone off the previous night,
most of them in this neighborhood, which is called
Teusaquillo, and it is one of the pleasantest in Bogotá.
—Alma Guillermoprieto

Flowering sietecueros trees:
How easily we married ourselves
to the idea of that bruised light
outside the window,
capillary
fibers of the linen,
stained wood of the door frame.
Deepening hallway.
Beyond
the stucco portal,
crushed purple.

At night, tinnitus
we thought,
the ringing after an explosion,
a frenzied inner ear axle squeal,
until I placed my stethoscope's bell
on the purpled ceiling:

Bats at roost
under the terracotta tiles,
each squeak a vector between mountains,
sicarios ricocheting through the dark.

"If you press your skull between the pillows,
it's like a lullaby."

At dawn our windows
imploded from the street.
Before the glaziers knocked, a breeze:
Blood-sweet draft of begonias
rising again from the iron grillwork
of our little yard.

Poema andino

after Paul Celan

Can you see the rooster's head,
freshly cut,
the beak still wanting to sing in the dirt?
Mounds of blue potatoes.
Grunting casually
the black hog—shiny
knot of rectum
spilled out above his testicles.
Purple and rust
kernels of corn
in straw baskets.
Smell of bus exhaust
before the quiet.
Above the highlands
moon the color of paper ash.
Faint seam of blood
in the fields, apron of wind, horsemint:
a human arm, brown and veined, is rising now
up through the circuitry of maize.

La gota fría

for Mike Sell

An infant spiked to a tree
through voice box and spine
in the dusty Colombian town of Segovia
I didn't imagine that

A beetle walks into the baby's
mouth for moisture
gray sky and leathery leaves

I have a wooden matchbox
fashioned as a small guitar
Its matchsticks are wax and burn
aquamarine   In Spanish
mostrar means *to show*

I don't know what that silence
sounds like
or what the hammer on the ground is thinking
In one ear
I hear caged lovebirds
inventing the monstrous world
In the other the cracked

throat of Emiliano Zuleta
It's the dry season
The old man's humming the vallenato
fingertips playing a box of air
window open
to the dark and empty kitchen

Águila y cóndor

He's walking through the stone stairs, carved man, standing, feathered burdens roped to his shoulders and back, teeth of yellow and blue corn, coca leaves cheek-pouched: mountain light on the old straw hat. Quena of bamboo. Yachac.

Torso of the bent man curves northeast, crescent, airy in spite of the stacked wool, glass, terracotta pipe, and kindling. He's walking through palisades, smaller rocks, arched wooden frames. He's walking through that woman on a rope bridge spanning the wide ridges.

In the middle of his polluted body, between mountains, is a gold and pink savannah. Pacha. She is shining. Look:

Eagle and condor are carrying them away.

Cholula

Fue un accidente
said the worker pedaling slowly past
on his rusted bike
a boy on the handlebars
poised as if on a femur of air
this moment of a dozen breaths
when the desert light is crushed
between lavender and auburn

On a walk a minute before
we never heard the sound of screeching brakes
nor the idle of the engine
before it moved away

The eyes from under the straw hat
were trained on me
as though I were a new priest
We fell silent
amid the small houses and tiendas
a farmer herding his cows with a blade-soft branch
the vast pyramid hidden as a hill

Fue un accidente
he repeated glancing back at us
moving away

The blond dog still warm
a pool of blood from the ear
dark and silvered by the moon

Sometimes I listen to a song six times

for Bessie Smith and Richard Morgan

We crash on that long, mesmerizing road
and I bleed like any Mississippi soul.

I could be a ghost or the crushed mouths
of wild orchids. But I don't want to die.

Baby, sometimes I listen to a song six times.
Baby, baby, mother knows I can bleed.

Snow's a ghost in my chest. Say I can fly.
Say I can sing.

Say, Oh no, Papa by the side of the road.
That's my arm

and gasoline:
my bloodless hand

cold as a dragonfly. Long old road,
it makes my love come down.

Sing, Long old road,
it makes my love come down.

If you could this summer, who would you kiss?

If you could this summer, where would you go?
Inside a watery mosque, tiny as roe.

If you could this summer, rain, how would you scroll?
Lizard feet cross a windshield, branch as they roll.

If you could this summer, what would you learn?
To sing through veins of vowels as they burn.

If you could this summer, tell me, who would you kiss?
The green woman in the maize, who flowers like this.

Poema without hands

Whatever it is that is wanting
is poema: her light blue sweater on the train.

The families in the unventilated
truck,

      the leeks
in the leek soup. The pal-

pitations whenever he reads
certain words: *alive, wild rat,*

Cocteau, acid, noose.
Her ring finger in the metal

lathe at work, Guevara's
hands from Bolivia, the

      painted frog from Boyacá,
drusen

accumulating in the macula of the painter's son.
The mountaintops near Caney Creek

in eastern Kentucky,
Atakapa her tongue and half her face

in shadow, the cistern on the beach where once their sweet
bones rocked, honeycombs in the eyes of the honeybee.

Whisper Beside Falling Bodies

I'll cut only the curling tip of your Verona hair

I'll tuck it in the hollow of the glass hand I blew
through the iron pipe in the dim garage, mice at my feet

I'll tell no one where I put it, not even
the quarrelsome woman in the antique locket,
white egret feathers and *hauteur* running down her throat

I'll say little to the mailman in the blue surgical gloves,
except, "Isn't it too late for that?"

If the cat scatters the penny-bright onion skins
over the kitchen floor,
I'll pretend to be too large for the room,

duck under the portals,
go outside into the night and climb the roof of the A-frame

Above fires sparking in drums,
I'll position the clear hand upturned in the sky,
so that it palms the moon, single ovary,

so that the blinking jet beyond the ridge of the Appalachians
threads the invisible wrist with fresh blood,

slipping through the copper vortex of your stolen hair

Acknowledgments

Earlier versions of the following poems first appeared in these publications:

The Cream City Review:

"What Baby Gertrude Heard" and "Whisper Beside Falling Bodies"

A Generation Defining Itself In its Own Words (MWE Publications):

"Long Time Ago in Chicago John Prine Used to Be My Friend's Mailman"

Hot Metal Bridge (electronic):

"The Sound of Glass is Unmistakable"

Joyful Noise: An Anthology of American Spiritual Poetry (Autumn House Press):

"Blue Dress of Chiquinquirá"

Lake Effect:

"La gota fría"

No Boundaries: Prose Poems by 24 American Poets (Tupelo Press):

"The Exegesis"

Ploughshares:

"Cage"

Seneca Review:

"Someone Complaining Around Here"

Sentence: A Journal of Prose Poetics:

"The other word for thesaurus"

The Southern California Anthology:

"Sometimes I listen to a song six times" and "West of Eliza Furnace"

TriQuarterly:

"Cholula" and "Soup for an Oligarch"

Ward 6 (electronic):

"Against Metaphor" and "At Sunrise, Oaxaca"

In addition, mil besos and thanks go to Janet Jennerjohn for her wise editorial work on this book and for being my true north. With great love we dedicate *Poema* to the memory of Betty Jennerjohn and Eddie Riggio.

About the Author

Maurice Kilwein Guevara was born in Belencito, Colombia, in 1961 and raised in Pittsburgh, Pennsylvania. He is Professor of English at the University of Wisconsin–Milwaukee, where he teaches in the MA and PhD programs in creative writing as well as in the Latino Studies Program. His first book of poetry, *Postmortem* (University of Georgia Press), won the National Contemporary Poetry Series Competition and was published in 1994. His second volume, *Poems of the River Spirit*, was published in the Pitt Poetry Series in 1996. His third collection, *Autobiography of So-and-so: Poems in Prose*, came out in 2001 in the Green Rose Series of New Issues Press. A dynamic presenter of his own work, Kilwein Guevara has given poetry performances and workshops in Mexico, Colombia, Costa Rica, Spain, Cuba, and throughout the United States. His work has appeared in *Poetry, Parnassus, Ploughshares, Exquisite Corpse, Kenyon Review, TriQuarterly*, and *The Journal of the American Medical Association*. His poetry has been anthologized in *Touching the Fire: Fifteen Poets of Today's Latino Renaissance* (Anchor/Doubleday), *American Poetry: The Next Generation* (Carnegie Mellon University Press), *The New American Poets: A Bread Loaf Anthology* (University Press of New England), and *No Boundaries: Prose Poems by 24 American Poets* (Tupelo Press), among others. He has served on the board of directors of the Association of Writers and Writing Programs and was the first Latino to be elected as its president. He is married to the poet Janet Jennerjohn, and they have two sons.